BLIMPS

FLYING MACHINES

Kelly Baysura

Rourke Publishing LLC

www.rourkepublishing.com

PHOTO CREDITS:
© Courtesy of Good Year: Cover, pages 1, 4, 10, 12, 13, 17, 21
© Carnegie Library of Pittsburgh, PA: Page 8
© Courtesy of Kevin Pace: Page 15
© Courtesy of the Lighship Group: Page 18

About The Author:

Kelly Baysura graduated from Duquesne University in Pittsburgh, PA with a degree in Elementary Education. Kelly has taught grades K, 1, 4, and 5 and was most recently employed in the education field as a reading specialist.

EDITORIAL SERVICES:
Pamela Schroeder

Library of Congress Cataloging-in-Publication Data

Baysura, Kelly, 1970–
    Blimps / Kelly Baysura.
        p. cm. — (Flying machines)
    Includes bibliographical references and index
    ISBN 1-58952-002-5
    1. Airships—Juvenile literature. [1. Airships.] I. Title

TL650.5 .B395 2001
629.133'24—dc21

00-066523

Printed in the USA

TABLE OF CONTENTS

HELIUM

Have you ever wondered why some balloons float and others fall to the ground? The balloons that float are filled with a gas called **helium**. Helium is a lighter-than-air gas. Air is heavier than the helium. That's why helium balloons float. Blimps are like helium balloons.

A Good Year Blimp films a Pittsburgh Steelers football game at Three Rivers Stadium in Pittsburgh, PA.

LIGHTER THAN AIR

Blimps fly because they are lighter than air. Floating balloons and blimps are called "lighter-than-air aircraft". Lighter-than-air aircraft are filled with a special gas. Today this gas is helium. Helium is used because it is safe. People do not use **hydrogen** to fill balloons or blimps anymore. It is very **flammable** and has caused fires.

Blimps travel slowly making them great for sightseeing.

THE FIRST BLIMPS

In 1852 Henri Giffard built a sausage-shaped balloon. This balloon-like aircraft was known as a **zeppelin**, or blimp. These first blimps were as long as football fields. They used gas bags filled with hydrogen to make them rise. The aircraft moved using small steam engines. They also had rudders for steering.

One of the first airships built was powered by a bicycle.

WAR

Zeppelins were used in the Second World War. The Germans used zeppelins to drop bombs on England. After the war zeppelins were turned into **airliners**. They were used to carry passengers.

The US Navy used blimps to see and track enemy activity.

A blimp is about as long as a football field and needs a lot of space to take off and land. People used blimps to travel to faraway lands.

People get to see Good Year blimps up close at a blimp hanger and landing site.

A TERRIBLE ACCIDENT

Early blimps had many accidents. Some accidents were caused by bad weather. Some were caused by mechanical problems. Hydrogen gas caused others. People were worried about being safe in blimps.

A terrible accident occurred in 1937. The *Hindenburg* was the name of a German zeppelin. It crashed in flames in New Jersey. Hydrogen gas made the zeppelin catch on fire. This accident ended the use of blimps for carrying passengers.

The Hindenburgh

BLIMPS TODAY

Modern blimps have gone through some changes. The blimps that we sometimes see flying overhead use helium instead of hydrogen. Helium is not dangerous like hydrogen. The blimps cannot catch on fire very easily.

A blimp is like a large balloon floating through the air.

PARTS OF A BLIMP

Blimps float like balloons. The balloon part is called the **envelope**. The envelope is filled with helium. That's how blimps float. There are special air valves on blimps to release or add helium. If the blimp needs to go higher, the pilot adds helium. If it needs to go lower, the pilot releases helium to make the blimp heavier.

Blimps have engines to make them move. The engines are on both sides of the **gondola**. The gondola is the cabin under the envelope. It is where the pilot and co-pilot ride.

The gondola holds only a small number of people at one time.

HOW WE USE BLIMPS

Blimps do have engines, but they can't fly very fast. They are used for things like sightseeing and advertising. People can travel slowly and quietly on blimps. Blimps are no longer used for passenger travel. Airplanes can travel much faster.

These blimps fly low to get a good view of London.

Many companies use blimps to carry TV cameras or ads. Blimps are good for filming sporting events. They float slowly and quietly over the event. Have you ever seen a blimp fly over your house?

GLOSSARY

airliner (AYR ly ner) — a large passenger airplane

envelope (EN veh lohp) — the covering or outer layer of the blimp

flammable (FLAM eh buhl) — easily set on fire

gondola (GON deh luh) — a car that hangs under an airship and holds passengers

helium (HEE lee um) — a very light, colorless, odorless gas that will not burn

hydrogen (HY dro jen) — a colorless, odorless gas that burns easily

zeppelin (ZEP eh lin) — a large cigar-shaped airship with separate compartments filled with gas

INDEX

FURTHER READING

Find out more about blimps with these helpful books and information sites:
•www.letsfindout.com/aviation   •www.nasm.edu
•www.hotairship.com   •www.goodyear.com

Jennings, Terry. *Planes, Gliders, Helicopters, and Other Flying Machines.* Kingfisher Books, 1993.
Kerrod, Robin. *Amazing Flying Machines.* Alfred A. Knofp, 1992